BRITAIN IN OLD

BRIDLINGTON

IAN AND MARGARET SUMNER

ALAN SUTTON PUBLISHING LIMITED

Alan Sutton Publishing Limited
Phoenix Mill · Far Thrupp · Stroud
Gloucestershire · GL5 2BU

First published 1995

Cover photographs: (front) a publicity stunt in Prince Street, 1922; (back) the Spa from the entrance to the gardens.

British Library Cataloguing in Publication Data.
A catalogue record for this book is available from the British Library.

ISBN 0-7509-0762-2

Typeset in 9/10 Sabon.
Typesetting and origination by
Alan Sutton Publishing Limited.
Printed in Great Britain by
Hartnolls, Bodmin, Cornwall.

Contents

Introduction

'Be mine the task in grateful lays,
To sing, O charming Quay, thy praise!'

James Coates, 1805

The seaside town of Bridlington is well known, not only within the East Riding, but all over Yorkshire and the North Midlands, as a holiday destination. Of course it was not always so; for many years the twin settlements of Bridlington and Bridlington Quay were nothing but small East Riding towns.

Bridlington, whose name comes from 'Berhtel's farmstead', was an Anglian settlement at the side of the Roman road to Flamborough, and it probably would have stayed quite small, had not Gilbert de Gant, the lord of the manor, decided to found a priory on his land early in the twelfth century. The Priory received permission to hold a market and fair in 1200 and it was around this site that the town grew up. It grew only slowly – even by 1334 it was still smaller than the nearby villages of Kilham and Hunmanby. At the same time a small fisherman's settlement, called Castleburn, was founded by the sea, around the mouth of the Gypsey Race stream. Bridlington began to prosper in the fifteenth century, following the canonisation of one of the priors, John of Thwing. The Priory thus became a centre of pilgrimage, even attracting King Henry V, who came to give thanks for his victory at Agincourt in 1415.

While the Priory was the foundation of the medieval town's prosperity, however, it was also the reason for its decline. The Priory was dissolved – and demolished – in 1537, in the wake of the failed Pilgrimage of Grace rebellion, and the town's fortunes plummeted. With so little income in the town, it was the settlement by the sea, now known as Burlington or Bridlington Quay, which expanded. The alternative name, Burlington, appears to have its origins in the flexible spelling of the time – from Bridlington to Brillington to Burlington – and was commonly used throughout the sixteenth and seventeenth centuries, and even into the eighteenth. Even so Bridlington had been used as early as 1080. The Crown was the lord of the manor in the early sixteenth century, but was forced to spend great sums of money keeping both town and harbour in good repair. It therefore gave the manor to Sir George Ramsey, King James I's favourite, but he had no use for it either, and in what became known as the Great Town Deed it was sold to a group of thirteen townsmen, who became known as the Lords Feoffees.

During the Civil War the port was a convenient point of entry for Royalist ships running the Parliamentarian blockade to bring in arms and supplies from the Continent, particularly from the Netherlands. By the 1660s the port had so grown in importance that, when war broke out with the Dutch, it was bombarded by the Dutch fleet in 1666. The reply was to build a fort on the north side of the harbour in the following year, and a smaller battery on the south side. Both were eventually lost to erosion at the start of the nineteenth century, but are commemorated in the names Garrison Street and Fort Terrace.

People were dipping a toe in the chilly waters of the North Sea from the 1770s at least, but Bridlington did not become really fashionable as a resort until the visits of the Duke of Leeds in 1808, and the Duke of Newcastle five years later. In 1821, it was being said of the Quay that, in the last fifty years, it had 'from an inconsiderable village become a neat, lively and populous town'. In fact, the population was a little over 3,000. All the prosperity that came with these new visitors went to the Quay and not to the Old Town. Ten years later, the latter was described as having 'narrow, crooked and irregular streets', in contrast to the 'remarkably gracious' Quay, with its 'modern and neatly-built' houses. The town had everything the refined visitor could require: bathing machines, sea breezes, coastal scenery, shipping in the bay, nearby places of historic interest, inns (165 of them in 1846), shops, venues for playing billiards and cards, baths, and a beach full of shells, stones and fossils. The season ran from mid-June to early October, and, according to T. Allen in *History of Yorkshire* (vol. 4), attracted visitors from Hull (19 per cent of all visitors in 1843), the rest of Yorkshire (61 per cent) and even the north Midlands (16 per cent). As one visitor commented in 1858, 'Bridlington attracts numbers of that class of visitor for whom Hornsea is too quiet and Scarborough too gay'.

What changed the nature of the town was the coming of the railway in 1846, connecting Bridlington with Hull. The importance of shipping to the town's economy had been slowly declining for some years and the easy transport of goods by rail, together with the growth of steam shipping, almost finished the coastal trade completely. These could have been dark days for the town, since it became reliant on the tourist trade alone, but even so it prospered and began to expand. The two communities of Old Town and Quay began to move towards each other and much building was carried out on the north side of the Quay. A start was made on the Alexandra Hotel in 1863 and on the Sea Wall Parade in 1866; the Crescent was laid out in 1869, and building on the Beaconsfield Estate commenced in the same year. By the end of the following decade, the sea wall had been extended with the addition of the Alexandra Wall, estates of new houses were being built inland from the Quay, and, with the erection of the first permanent bridge over the Gypsey Race in 1882, new building started to the south of the town as well.

More changes came with the introduction of day trip tickets and cheap period returns on the railways in the early 1870s. On August Bank Holiday Monday in 1879 there were 5,000 visitors; on Whit Monday in 1885 there were 2,000 day trippers from Hull alone. Some thought that the trippers, 'some of whom were the rougher sort', spoiled the town, but still they kept coming. In 1867 there were 228 hotels and boarding houses to accommodate the visitors; by 1892, this had risen to 458; by 1913 it had reached a massive 922. And facilities had to be provided to entertain the visitor. After some false starts, the South Cliff Sea Wall was completed in 1896 and was renamed the

Spa Wall after the opening of the Spa in that year; this was followed by the building of the Hydro in Marine Drive two years later. These were complemented on the north side by the Floral Pavilion, built in 1904, and the Grand Pavilion two years later. Here, visitors were treated to concerts and recitals by many artists, both national and local. In contrast, a project to build a pleasure pier on the North Sands came to nothing. All this activity had its effect on the local population too. In 1891 the total population of both the Old Town and the Quay was 6,840; in 1901, it had increased to 9,528; by 1911, it was 14,334. In other words, it had more than doubled in twenty years. By the 1920s, it was estimated that as much as a quarter of the working population of the town was connected with the tourist industry. Another benefit to the town arising from this prosperity was its incorporation as a borough in 1899.

After the end of the Second World War, changing habits and uncertain weather saw the beginning of the decline of the traditional English seaside holiday. The most common visitor became the day-tripper, and less than a sixth of holiday-makers stayed for more than a week. Nothing could, however, detract from Bridlington's magnificent natural setting, and it remains a popular resort with a welcome for everyone.

THE OLD TOWN

Two views of the Priory across Church Green. Above is the church as it was before the restoration work of 1878–9 by Sir George Gilbert Scott. It has shorter towers and a small octagonal cupola dating from the eighteenth century on the south-west tower. Below we see the effect of Scott's work, familiar to us today. The building on the left (shown more clearly in the top picture) is the Infants' National School, opened in 1857 and closed in 1910. At this time there were 160 children at the school.

The doors of the Priory. The date is unknown, although the boy's tall top hat suggests a date in the 1860s or 1870s. The identity of the boy is also not known.

The Priory from High Green. High, Low and Church Greens were all used as the location of sheep and cattle markets at one time. These markets later became pleasure fairs, and the Charter Fair was held here until 1973.

High Green and Pinfold Street from the Priory tower. In the background is Burlington Council School, opened in 1910 to replace the National Schools. There were 526 children attending in 1912.

High Green, 17 July 1919. A procession assembles for the finale of the Peace Day celebrations. This part of the celebrations consisted of a historical pageant of Bridlingtonians through the ages. These are the Ancient Britons and Romans. The three shire horses which pulled the chariot were singled out for special mention in the press.

Sergeant-Major William Henry Morris, of 1 Albert Cottages, Priory Walk. He was a member of the local Artillery Volunteers. The stars and lozenge on his cuff testify that he was a long-serving member of the corps, having seen over thirty years' service with the Volunteers, who were the forerunners of the Territorial Army. He also wears the unusual four-pointed star above his rank badge, indicating that he was deemed 'proficient' as a sergeant.

The Bayle. Once the gatehouse of the Priory, it is the only building, apart from the church, which survives from the old monastery. Houses went right up to the Bayle until quite recently, when they were demolished for road widening. The triangular block on the left had, however, disappeared by 1911. The building on the right served as a Baptist chapel from 1714 until its demolition in 1873. The coat of arms over the gate is that used by the monastery. The shuttered house became the Bull and Sun Hotel.

The police station in Nungate (now Sewerby Road). Built in 1843–4 it was near the junction with Pinfold Street. It was closed in 1881 on the opening of a new station on Ashville Street and is now the site of a block of flats. Local children used to call the building the 'Bucket House' because of the resemblance of its windows to an upturned bucket.

7 Sewerby Road. This was once the home of the Means family, who had a fruiterer's business. The building itself is made from a combination of chalkstone, brick, stone and cobbles, and has Yorkshire sash windows (which open horizontally). It has now been demolished.

Cottages on Nungate (now Sewerby Road). Note that the one on the right is made from cobbles, but with stone quoins. All were demolished in the late 1940s for road widening.

The twin cemetery chapels, Sewerby Road. Extravagant Victoriana, they were built in 1879 to the designs of Alfred Smith of Nottingham. The cemetery was opened, and the chapels consecrated, in 1883 as a private concern. It was taken over by the corporation in 1904.

The old workhouse, Marton Road. The first mention of a workhouse in Bridlington is in 1743, but this building was built in 1847–8 to the designs of Charles Tilney of York. It served thirty local townships within the Poor Law Union. It has since been converted to a nursing home, and named Burlington House.

The High Street. The building with the columns around the door is the Dominican Convent School. It was originally built as a house, in about 1825, but was turned into a school in 1930. On the right is Craven House. This was built in about 1670, but the front was added in 1806. It once belonged to William Horsely and his wife Ann (née Nesfield), and extended as far as North Back Lane (now part of Scarborough Road).

Sawdons the butcher's, 32 High Street. It is decorated for the coronation of King Edward VII in 1902. The man in the white apron is the owner, William Sawdon (1861–1910), who was Mayor of Bridlington from 1905 to 1908. He is remembered in a bust on the Memorial Drinking Fountain on Baylegate.

45 High Street, 1947. The shop of Edmund's printers and stationers dates from 1693, but the elegant bowed window are later additions (*c.* 1790).

64 High Street, 1947. The house was built in the eighteenth century. Next door is the Board Inn, belonging to Charles Rose, a Malton brewery. It is formed from two buildings, one dating from the seventeenth century; the other from the eighteenth.

70 High Street, *c.* 1890. The display of William Milner, ironmonger, includes pots, pans and kettles. Note the delicate street light on the right.

67 High Street, *c.* 1890. A crowd outside another ironmonger's, Edwin Dale, watch the camera watching them. Dale seems to specialise in oil lamps if his window display is anything to go by.

The proclamation of King Edward VII, Market Place, 1901. The building occupied by Smith's Seed Merchants, Centre House, was built on the site of the old market cross in about 1821, and was demolished in 1913. In the background on the right are troopers of the Yorkshire Hussars Yeomanry in what must have been their last public duty in the area before the raising of the East Riding Regiment.

Market Place. The town's market was held here until about 1910, when it was superseded by those in King and Prince Streets. On the right is the Corn Exchange, built in 1824. It has since been demolished, and in 1971 was replaced by a house. Further up the street is the Nag's Head public house. In the centre is a horse bus. Omnibuses, owned by Reuben Williamson of Quay Road, ran half-hourly between the Old Town and the Quay.

Blue Bell Entry, Market Place, 1947. It was here that the town stocks and pillory stood. Note the rounded bay windows on the building to the right: these were a feature of many early nineteenth-century Bridlington houses, especially in the Quay.

The opening of the National Reserve Club House, 31 March 1913. Situated opposite the Corn Exchange, the opening was performed by Major-General Burton. Also present in this photograph are Dr Hill (the mayor), Percival Hewitt, C. Harland, Jack Wright senior, J.B. Purvis and T. Boynton. The Reserve was an organisation of ex-soldiers who could form a trained pool of men in time of war. In Bridlington there were about 350 men, formed into three companies.

Westgate, looking away from the town. On the right, at the corner of the Market Place, is Barclays Bank, built in about 1900. On the left are the current premises of the Midland Bank. Just visible behind the bank is the sign of the Old Star Inn, which is late seventeenth century in origin.

The Midland Bank's premises, 1947. This building was once the home of the Hebblethwaite family, who had a large estate in Bridlington and around Weaverthorpe. It was built in about 1675 and was converted into a bank in 1926.

The rear of the Avenues Hospital. It was originally built in 1714 as the home of the Prickett family, who had a large estate in this part of the county. It was named after an avenue of trees which now forms part of Westgate Park. The building served as an annexe for the grammar school, before becoming a hospital in 1932. Having lain derelict for a number of years it is now about to be converted into flats.

The corner of St John's Street and Kirkgate (which runs off to the right). On the left side is the end of Waterworks Street. These buildings, and many more on Waterworks Street, were demolished to make way for Scarborough Road – perhaps this is why the road is closed in the picture. Note all the advertisement posters on the wall to the left – 'Guinness for strength', 'Aah Bisto!', Camp Coffee, Oxo and Bovril – all remain household names to this day. The waterworks, after which the street was named, were built at the corner of Marton Lane and Mill Lane in 1865. They were taken over by the council in 1899.

An outing from Sledmere, 1909. In the background is the Priory Church Institute. The institute was opened, in 1885, in the former Methodist chapel on St John's Street (itself built in 1775). The building was sold in 1958 and is now a shop.

The original Zion chapel, St John's Street, *c.* 1885. It was built soon after 1700 but was subsequently altered and enlarged to accommodate a growing congregation. It is seen here after restoration. It was finally demolished in the early years of this century and the plot used as a Congregational burial ground.

St John's Street. Behind the trees on the left is The Elms. This was converted into the High School for Girls, which opened in 1905. The cottages on the left were demolished in 1906 to make way for the new Zion chapel, while those on the right were lost to road widening. The man on the left looks like a fisherman selling his catch direct to the public.

The Baptist chapel, Quay Road. It was built in 1874 to Samuel Musgrave's plans and seated 508. The scheme included a schoolroom, but this was not started until 1898. By 1985 the chapel had become unsafe and was demolished. The plot on the left is now the magistrate's court.

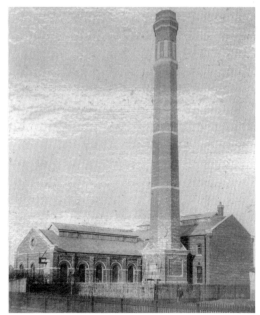

The corporation power station, Brett Street. Built in 1905, it continued in operation until 1935, when supplies were taken from the National Grid. Much of the electricity it supplied went to street lighting and to the public buildings at the Quay.

Fire Brigade personnel, June 1925. The Brigade was formed on a full-time basis in 1899, and consisted of a captain and eleven men. The fire station was in Portland Place, off St John's Street.

One of the Brigade's engines, *c.* 1930. The first engine in the town was bought in 1767. The Lords Feoffees later had two: one in the Old Town and one at the Quay. The first belonging to the Municipal Brigade was bought in 1912, and was kept at the station on Portland Street.

Beneath all the flags the outline of a fire engine can just be distinguished. It looks like one of those which formerly belonged to the Lords Feoffees. The photograph may show the Peace Day celebrations of 1919, or perhaps a carnival.

Bridlington Grammar School. The date of the school's foundation is unknown, but it certainly existed as part of the Priory in 1200. It was forced to close in 1866, as the endowments did not produce sufficient income to maintain the school or to employ a competent teacher. It re-formed in 1894, with new endowments, and opened its doors in 1899; the opening ceremony was performed by Lord Herries. At that time the headmaster was Arthur Thornton MA; there were 150 boys attending, of whom about one third were boarders.

White Lodge. Called Rose Villa at the turn of the century, it had been bought by the Borough in 1925, perhaps because it occupied a site between the two halves of the Borough. The Old Town and the Quay were originally about a mile apart; the Lodge is about half-way between them. A number of departments were transferred here. A new building, designed by the Borough Architect, P.M. Newton, was built in 1932 at a cost of £34,000. The Lodge has since been demolished to make way for the present Town Hall.

The Lodge's ornamental gardens. After the new Town Hall was built, they were turned into a putting green. In the distance can be seen the power station chimney.

The first council meeting in the new Town Hall, May 1932. The mayor, Councillor Dew, is in the chair. The opening ceremonies began with a procession from Christ Church. Some 800 members of the public were invited inside, and were 'pleasantly surprised at the beauties of the building' (*Bridlington Free Press*). Previously, meetings had been held in the Victoria Rooms at the harbour side; these were burnt down in the following year.

The Recreation Ground. This cyclists' meeting included a contingent from Wakefield. Note the tricycle in the centre; it is probably a Quadrant. There were at least two cycling clubs in the town at the turn of the century, and annual cycling meets at Whitsun involved clubs from all over Yorkshire. A piece of land at the end of Olivers Lane was used as a recreation ground from 1884 and, until 1920, included a cycle track. It was enlarged by a gift of land from George Dukes and was subsequently named Dukes Park.

The staff of Bridlington station, 1895. Back row, left to right: M. Dickinson, -?-, Assistant Station Master Harrison, Station Master Shipman, Shipman's son, W. Scott, -?-, Vanman Sellers, -?-, F. Green. Middle row: ? Hetherington, Ticket Collector Robson, Porter Whiting, W. Clark, ? Bean, ? Robson, Ticket Collector Westell, ? Parker, -?-. Front row: ? Walker, -?-, -?-, ? Robson, -?-. The men's uniform is dark blue, with gold badges for the station master and red for the others.

Another group of station staff, 1900. The surnames of those pictured include Baker, Westell, Robson, Dove, Luther, Walker, Newlove, Bean, Taylor, Brompton, Sellers and Sawden.

Outside the station, July 1924. This is the old entrance to the station, built in 1849, on the path by the Town Hall gardens; the current entrance building was not built until 1912. This is a publicity call for Rupert Hazell's Concert Party. The Brighter Brid revue, which went 'with a merry swing throughout', played at the Grand Pavilion. Rupert Hazell played the phono-fiddle, whilst the other members of the company contributed piano duets, a banjulele band and songs.

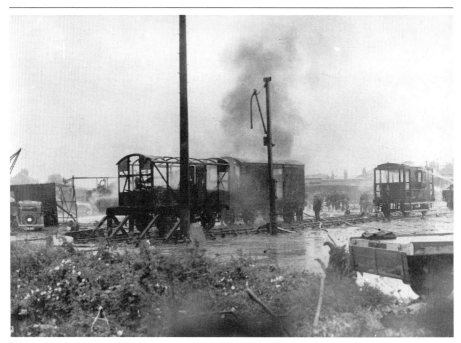

The aftermath of a German air raid, 1941. These burnt-out railway wagons were apparently carrying ammunition when they were hit.

Peace Day procession, 18 July 1919. It has reached the railway crossing on Quay Road. There were two processions that day: this one featured floats and the lifeboat, the other was of returned servicemen. Note the curious little donkey cart in the lead: the papers mention 'Dilly and Dally' in a convalescent donkey cart and this may be them.

THE QUAY

Peace Day procession, Quay Road. It is passing Jemison's auctioneer's and Nettleship's plumber's. Behind the two decorated carts is a pipe band and a Boys' or Church Lads' Brigade party.

Christ Church, at the corner of Quay Road and Prospect Street. The trees on the left are now long gone. The church was built in 1840–1 by Sir George Gilbert Scott and William Bonython Moffatt, enlarged in 1851, and the steeple added in 1859. In his *Recollections*, Scott calls the church 'his first and worst'; nevertheless it is a familiar sight to every holiday-maker, passing it in search of 'digs' on the way from the station.

The Fishermen's Sunday procession, Quay Road. It is passing Nettleship's and the Cricketer's Arms. The procession commemorated the Great Gale of 1871, when thirty ships were wrecked in the bay, and seventy men lost their lives. It started at the harbour, and finished at the Sailors' Monument at the Priory. The tradition ceased during the 1970s.

The Corporation Electricity showrooms on the corner of Quay Road and Victoria Road. They were opened in May 1939 and destroyed by enemy action less than two years later, in February 1941.

The Manor House. Built in 1830 at the corner of Beck Hill and Manor Street, it was once the residence of Dr A. Whitaker, who moved to Quay Road in 1920. The house was taken over by Dr Kirkland, but it was demolished in 1928, to make way for Lloyd's Bank. Note the street organ in the centre of the picture.

Manor Street. Is this a funeral? The wagons appear to be carrying flag-draped boxes. In the background is 6 Manor Street, which is now a bank, but was once the town house of Sir Henry Boynton of Burton Agnes. It was built in 1810, and has rounded bay windows and an elaborate porch.

Swallow's, 3 Manor Street, 1926. It displays a fine array of fruit: as the sign in the window says, 'Nothing but the best'. Note the scales on the right.

The original Wesleyan chapel. It was built on Cliff (now Chapel) Street in 1798 and was enlarged several times in the succeeding years, lastly in 1840, as the inscription on the building shows. It was demolished in 1873, and replaced by the current, more imposing, building further down the street.

A very smart group of boys from the Wesleyan Day School, Princess Street, 1898. There were 208 children of all ages by 1908, but numbers fell off in the years before the First World War, and the school closed in 1915. The infants' department still stands and is now known as the Princess Rooms. The older man on the right might be A. Humphreys, teacher.

A Fishermen's Sunday parade, King Street, c. 1925. Note the two newsreel cameras, one at least from Movietone, mounted on the tops of the vans, recording the event for posterity.

The Argenta Meat Company, King Street, 1947. There are still references to food rationing in the windows. Meat rationing was first introduced in 1940. Restrictions were gradually eased from 1948 onwards, but it was not until 1954 that meat was freely available. This building later became the extension to Binns' shop.

The opening of the new Public Library, King Street, by Councillor Dew, 1937. The building had previously been the York City and County Bank, and was built in 1897–8. Despite some public pressure, the council did not adopt the 1850 Public Libraries Act, which permitted councils to raise a rate for library purposes, until 1925. The first library was on Quay Road in the town's information bureau by the railway station.

King Street, looking towards Manor Street. On the left is the King's Arms public house, whose licensee was Robert Williamson. Next to it, further up the street, are the premises of Jane Rowntree, Grocer and Provision Dealer.

King Street. The blacksmith's is in the cottage in the centre. The first shop from the right with a sunblind is Speck's the butchers.

King Street. There are no fewer than three establishments offering a shave.

Queen House, Queen Street. Queen Henrietta Maria was supposed to have spent the night here in February 1643, when she brought ashore a convoy of arms and supplies from the Netherlands to aid the Royalist cause during the Civil War. The building later became the Oberon pub.

Bridge Street, from Hilderthorpe Road. The road was widened in 1903. On the right are the premises of Henry Musk, who continued to have a shop on the widened road; on the left is Weldon's boot factors.

Bridge Street. The widening operations are taking place. The culvert, built in 1882 to carry the Gypsey Race, is visible on the left. Note the large Quaker Oats advertisement on the wall of John Ainsworth's fishmonger's.

A fine Georgian house, Prince Street. On the left is the post office and William Headley's chemist's shop. Almost half of the house was demolished, in the nineteenth century, and the end windows replaced by bays on the upper floors – not to the building's advantage (as can be seen in the next picture).

The market, Prince Street. In front of the now-altered Georgian house are carriers from Nafferton and Barmston and a small horse-bus. The man in the centre wearing the top hat is Anthony Waite, the town's last Bellman and Toll Collector, serving from 1888 until 1901, when the post was abolished. His uniform was blue with red facings and silver lace. A market had been held in King Street since at least 1869; there was also a fish market in Queen Street. By the 1890s these had both become general markets, held in King and Prince Streets. The latter had ceased by 1949.

A busy Prince Street. In the centre of the street, wagonettes wait to take holiday-makers to Sewerby and Flamborough.

Prince Street. Granthams, the owners of the Universal Café (right), had opened a second establishment on Garrison Street (misspelt on their sign) and were to open a third on the Esplanade. A cab waits outside the Britannia Hotel. The building was demolished in 1941, after a German air raid, and the site is now occupied by a block of flats.

Prince Street, looking towards King Street, 1890s. In the background, a four-wheeled cab, of a type known as a 'growler', turns towards Queen Street.

Harry White's Oyster Saloon, 26 Prince Street, 1920s. It is only relatively recently that oysters have become a rich man's dish. As Sam Weller remarked, in Charles Dickens's *Pickwick Papers*, 'Poverty and oysters always seem to go together.'

The Cock and Lion, Prince Street. A John Smith's house, it had an extremely fine painted sign on the wall and ornamental animals on the roof. Ye Olde Oak Room, advertised on the wall outside, was a fine wood panelled room. Note how the landlord, H.V.H. Turner, advertises his Wakefield origins, no doubt to appeal to West Riding holiday-makers. The building was demolished after being damaged in the Blitz. In the 1960s it was replaced by a blandly anonymous building, still called the Cock & Lion.

John Bull's rock shop, Prince Street, 1929. Rock is one of the essentials of the seaside holiday, and there looks to be plenty of it about here.

A publicity stunt, Prince Street, July 1922. This clever costume was to advertise a forthcoming attraction at The Lounge café-theatre (also known as The Oriental Lounge). By their expressions, however, some onlookers do not seem that keen.

The aftermath of a German air raid, Prince Street, August 1940. The shop on the left is Woolworth's 3*d* and 6*d* Stores; on the right is Foley's Café and Restaurant.

A holiday group on the steps, Prince Street, 1921. The Victoria Rooms are on the right, above the Bluebird Café.

The Victoria Rooms on fire, 22 September 1933. The fire broke out early in the morning, probably in the refreshment rooms. It spread quickly, and a column of sparks 150 ft high was soon visible, even from Hull and Scarborough. Both fire engines attended, and the fire was finally put out at about 4.15 a.m.

The final end of the Victoria Rooms. They were built as public rooms in 1846, for concerts and meetings, and included a newsroom, reading and billiard rooms. Among those who played there were the young Charlie Chaplin and the original D'Oyly Carte opera company. It was also the town's first cinema. The rooms served as Bridlington's Town Hall from 1893 until the present one was built in 1932. After the fire in 1933 the ruins were too dangerous to be left and were demolished. The site has since been levelled.

The New Inn, Cross Street. The road was widened in 1905, and one of the main casualties of the work was this public house. It belonged to the Woodlesford-based Bentley's Yorkshire Breweries, and was run at this time by W.P. Hawkins.

Cross Street, *c.* 1908. The road-widening has been completed and the New Inn rebuilt, but the cottages behind have been totally removed. The 'largest retailers in England' – as appears on the wall on the left at the end of King Street – are Stead & Simpson, the shoe shop.

A clearance sale at Batchelor's, Cross Street, September 1924.

The carnival, Cross Street, 1923.

The carnival, 1923. Everyone is in black-face. Their identity is not known, but they all appear to be carrying small cones and may be a kazoo band. Such bands were very popular around the time of the First World War.

The Promenade, corner of Chapel and Cliff Streets, 1892. Samuel Anderson's premises are on the left; he moved away not long after this date. On the left also is the office of the *Bridlington and Quay Gazette*, a local newspaper, which ran between 1874 and 1914. Cheapside is on the right, and behind that are the Wholesale and Retail Cheap Furnishing Showrooms.

Cheapside, the Promenade, late 1940s. The row of shops was demolished in 1950, and has since been replaced by modern shops.

Burrell's Promenade Mews Riding School, advertised 'High class hacks and hunters' as well as riding lessons and 'carriages of every description'. The chimney at the rear was part of Simpson's brewery. The site became the East Yorkshire bus depot.

The Promenade, 1902. The shops are celebrating the coronation of King Edward VII. They include Braithwaite's milliner's and Gawthorn's stationer's. The newspaper hoardings are advertising the latest list of visitors to the resort, the Test Match, and an article on the Salvation Army and the King.

The Promenade, looking north. The corner of Marlborough Terrace is on the right. On the left is the United Methodist church built in 1872 to seat 500. It was deregistered in 1958 and demolished. Almost opposite it is the Trinity Congregational chapel, built in 1877 on the site of a skating rink. It was rebuilt two years later to seat 700. It is now a shop.

Captain J.B. Purvis, centre, flanked by his two sons. Purvis was a chemist, with a shop on the Promenade at the Princess Terrace corner. He was also an officer in the 5th (Territorial) Battalion of the Green Howards. At this time his elder son (on the left) was in Cambridge University OTC, and his younger, George, in the Grammar School Cadet Corps. George Purvis was killed at Passchendaele, serving as a captain with his father's regiment.

Jefferson's fruiterer's and florist's, the Promenade, junction with Princess Terrace. From the signs in the window, Jefferson's sold tea and Cadbury's chocolate as well.

The Promenade. Edith Myers and her sister Mary sit in a neat donkey carriage.

Ripley's garage, the Promenade. It is near the site of the East Yorkshire bus station. Herbert Ripley moved from Leeds in 1913 and opened premises in Rope Walk, before moving here just after the First World War. His business moved again, in 1934, to Hamilton Road, where it remains. If only Ford cars were £110 today!

The Promenade, near Victoria Terrace, 1860s. The Promenade was known by locals as The Lane for a long time. This view shows it before Holy Trinity church was built in 1871.

The Promenade, 1912. The owner, T. Tallentire, is wearing the light coat; the man second from the left is his assistant, M.G. Sampson. It is undoubtedly a fine display of produce, and one suspects that food hygiene regulations would prevent it today.

The Beaconsfield Hotel, Albion Terrace. In the background is Holy Trinity church, built in 1871, by the Revd Yarburgh Lloyd Greame. By the 1880s, the average attendance in summer was 1,100. In front of the hotel are Mary Knaggs and her donkeys. The Knaggs family had a livery stable on the Promenade; it later became a garage.

The leafy entrance to St Anne's Convalescent Home, Flamborough Road. It was opened in 1878 by Captain E. Barnes. Bombed in 1941 during a German air raid, the site remained vacant until 1961, when twelve almshouses – St Anne's Houses – were built. A further eight were built four years later.

St Anne's Road, *c.* 1937. The Convalescent Home is in the distance, near the large trees. The south side of the road, in the foreground, was still undeveloped at this time.

Windmill, Bempton Lane. It was built in 1823 by Moses Dukes, and was known as New, or Dukes's Mill, to distinguish it from the others in the town, situated along the Gypsey Race. It was still in use in 1913, but closed some time soon after that.

Beck Hill, from the bridge over the Gypsey Race. The spire of Christ Church is in the background. The buildings in the centre were later demolished to make way for Palace Avenue.

Hilderthorpe Road, after a German air raid on the night of 10/11 July. These buildings were once shops and the Cozy Corner Hotel.

Austin K2 ambulances. Bought by public subscription, they were handed over to the Army on 26 July 1940 as part of Bridlington's war effort.

Ozone Hotel, Windsor Crescent, 1935. Aircraftman T.E. Shaw, better known as Lawrence of Arabia, was billeted here when he was serving with the RAF detachment at the harbour during the 1920s.

West Street, with Neptune and South Streets on the right. The Board School is in the distance. The school was opened in 1882 and closed in 1953 when Hilderthorpe County Primary School replaced it.

Recruits, 1914. The young man in the centre appears to have come straight off the farm, with his double-breasted waistcoat, corduroy trousers and leggings. If the men were destined for Kitchener's new armies, then they would have probably ended up in one of seven service battalions raised by the Green Howards during the First World War. The Recruiting Office in the background with its Royal Navy posters was the Trinity House headquarters, at the bottom of West Street.

A procession to celebrate the coronation of George V was made through the town in 1911. This float possibly represented 'Africa', if the elephant is anything to go by, although 'India' is almost as likely.

Another view of the procession. It is crossing the railway bridge on Hilderthorpe Road. The men in white, and those immediately behind them, are members of a friendly society, probably the Druids. Behind them is a band, and, in the distance, mounted men of D Squadron of the East Riding Yeomanry.

Cardigan Road. In contrast to the streets north of the harbour, this area was quite slow to be developed. There was little building until the 1870s, and even then the financial difficulties of the developers and the lack of sea defences meant that there was no real growth until the 1890s, and the building of the Spa.

Kingston Road, *c.* 1943. A Sherman tank of the 1st Polish Armoured Division is brought to a halt by a policeman on point duty. The Wolds were used as a training area for Polish and Free French troops. The original caption reads: 'Just to make it known that the Army are not in sole control.' Perhaps it is only a semi-jocular reference to the all-encompassing nature of the war effort.

THE SOUTH SANDS

Carnaby Temple. This folly, built in the eighteenth century by Sir William Strickland of Boynton Hall, was used briefly as a look-out post during the Second World War.

Canvassing for votes in Bessingby, c. 1910. George Rennard, sitting in the car on the right, was first elected a borough councillor in 1901 and represented Hilderthorpe. Motor cars were more widely available in 1910, but even so, canvassing by car must have been something of an innovation. Rennard later became an alderman of the town.

Laying the foundation stone, St Magnus's church, Bessingby, 1893. The new church replaced an older foundation, St Mary Magdalen's, which had fallen into disuse. The group includes the vicar, Revd J.A. Pride. The church includes several memorials to the Wright family, who lived at Bessingby Hall.

Laying out sea defences, South Beach. Pembroke Terrace is in the background. A private attempt was made to build a sea wall in 1879 but it failed; the wall was eventually completed by the council in 1896. The railway appears to be one built to transport construction material from the harbour to the site. The rocks are the site of the future Spa.

Beach scene, pre-1914. The white Spa Theatre stands out clearly against the rest of the town. The windbreaks carry advertisements for Dunn's sand shoes. F. Dunn and Sons, who were based at Driffield, had a shop at 6 Prince Street, Bridlington, and another at York.

Marine Parade, 1920s. The area around Marine Parade, Horsforth Avenue and Cardigan Road was laid out in the last years of the nineteenth century, after the Spa and its sea wall had been completed.

South Marine Drive, showing the back of the Spa (right).

The back of the Spa (behind the fence on the left), looking towards Horsforth Avenue. The building with the ornate balcony is called Kingston House, and the shop underneath it is Budden's Stores.

The Spa, *c.* 1900. The boating pool is in the foreground with the Spa Theatre behind. Note the Chinese lanterns in the flower borders. The theatre later burnt down in October 1906 and the damage was estimated to be around £4,000. The rebuilt theatre and Opera House was opened by the actress Mrs Maud Beerbohm-Tree in July 1907.

The Spa, *c.* 1900. The Spa and Gardens were first opened in July 1896, when there was a concert by Herr Meyer Lutz's band, which was to be the resident orchestra. German band leaders were much in demand at this time because of the excellent musical training given to musicians in the German Army. The section on the right formed Field's Oriental Café, offering coffee and light refreshments 'of every description' and of the 'finest quality'.

Herr Julius Kändt and his band, 1910. Waxed and curled moustaches seem to be the rule, following the example of the conductor himself. At the end of the season, Herr Kändt was presented with a gold medal and a silver cake stand as well as other gifts, and was given a benefit concert for his part in doing 'so much towards reviving the somewhat decadent fortunes of the New Spa'. He was re-engaged for the next year. The band became the resident orchestra at the Spa in the years before the First World War.

The visit of the Lord Mayor of London, Walter Morgan, who came to re-open the Royal Prince's Parade extension in 1906. Here the procession is nearing the Spa. The nearest coach holds the civic regalia – the mace is visible sticking out of the window. Also visible in the foreground are some of the escort, troopers of the East Riding Yeomanry.

Another view of the procession, possibly at the corner of Neptune Street and Pembroke Terrace. The Lord Mayor stayed with W.B. Jameson of The Avenue. Many other guests, for the party also included the sheriffs, their ladies and the principal officers of the City, were accommodated at the Alexandra Hotel; the servants were placed at the Black Lion on the High Street.

Lord Mayor's procession, Spa Gardens. Morgan moved on to the Spa after opening the Parade extension. He then went to Flamborough, where the villagers had spelt out 'Welcome Lord Mayor' and 'Welcome to Flamborough' in chalk stones.

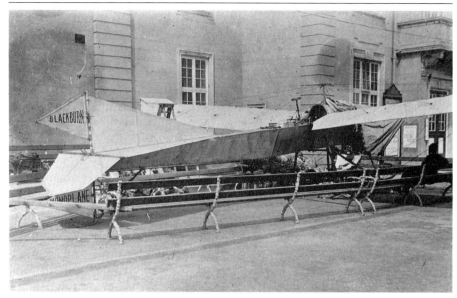

A Blackburn Mercury monoplane, July 1912. Bridlington's first aeroplane was flown by its owner, Jack Brereton. He made several flights over the sea front, taking off from the sands and the golf course, before poor weather curtailed the displays. Robert Blackburn (1885–1955), a native of Leeds, started his own aircraft company in 1910, at 18 Spencer Place, Leeds. He opened a second works at Brough, on the banks of the Humber, in 1916, and this became the main factory in 1928–9. It is still an aircraft factory, belonging to British Aerospace.

Building the Spa Royal Hall, 1926. The old Glass Dome was demolished to make way for a new concert hall, which included a sprung dance floor.

The Spa Royal Hall, 1932. Fire was spotted in the hall, just before 5 a.m., by a ship in the bay, and it raised the alarm. The Borough Fire Brigade brought both its motor and its horse-drawn appliances. There was some confusion at the scene and this led to the firefighters going to the Marine Drive side of the building, whereas the fire had broken out on the sea-wall side. The Spa band lost all its instruments, but the flames were stopped from spreading to the theatre next door.

Apple Pie Cottage, c. 1890. This stood on a site near the corner of the current Pembroke Terrace and Horsforth Avenue, near an iron-rich chalybeate spring – perhaps the one that gave the Spa its name. Living here at this time was Rosamund Broadbent, a native of Horsforth (near Leeds), her three sons and a daughter. She is probably one of the women standing in the doorway. The man on the right is a postman. Mrs Broadbent gave her occupation as a lodging-house keeper.

A rather glum-looking Princess Mary, 7 September 1928. The princess (daughter of King George V and mother of the present Earl of Harewood) is escorted by the mayor, Councillor Gray. She visited Bridlington to open the extension to the Spa sea wall. It was named Princess Mary Parade in her honour. After the opening ceremony she also visited the Lloyd Hospital.

The finished Spa Royal Hall, rebuilt after the 1932 fire.

The Spa from the entrance to the gardens. Note that entrance to the gardens was not free – a daily ticket cost 6d. The hoardings on the left advertise Herr Kändt's band, as well as Harry Leslie's production of *The Gay Lieutenants*.

The visit of Sir Alan Cobham, August 1929. The group is pictured on the Spa steps. Back row, left to right: G. Melom, ? Gray, ? Dick, -?-, C.R. Dunn. Front row: -?-, C.H. Gray (the mayor), the mayor's wife, Sir Alan Cobham, ? Storr and E. Lambert. Cobham (1894–1973) was an intrepid pioneer flyer, achieving many long-distance flying feats around the world. He also invented the modern method of air-to-air refuelling. He was on a national tour to make the country more 'air-minded', and to encourage towns like Bridlington to build their own airports.

Section Four

THE HARBOUR

The Sailors' Bethel, Clough Wharf, 1947. It had opened in 1934 in the former Albert Hall dance hall, which itself had previously been a warehouse.

Fisherwomen knitting at the harbourside. In the rear is the first Seamen's Bethel, built from corrugated iron. It stood until 1892, when it was demolished to make way for harbour improvements.

The harbour, north side. The view is towards what was to become Langdale's Wharf, at the west end of the harbour. The boats lined up here are all fishing cobles. There were some 300 boats fishing off Bridlington in 1902, but only eighty-four belonged to the town. Of these only a handful could be described as 'first class' and suitable for work in deeper waters.

Gutting the catch. The fishing fleets of Scotland and north-east England followed the migrating herrings southwards down the coast, and brought their own gutters with them. Each fish curer employed several gangs of his own gutters to clean and pack the fish into barrels of salt ready for transportation. The women were all either native Gaelic speakers from the north of Scotland, or from the area around Seahouses on the Northumberland coast.

The harbour, north side. The view looks along the course of the Gypsey Race.

Spring Pump slipway, Prince Street. In 1811 a tidal spring was discovered here and it was used to supply fresh water to this part of the Quay. It was still in use as late as 1880, before eventually being replaced by the water company's piped water.

The slipway at the end of Prince Street. In the distance is Prince Street; on the right are the Victoria Rooms. The whole block on the right has now disappeared.

The corner of Prince Street. During the 1920s the building was noted for its prominent advertisement for Brigham's photographic shop (Mr Snaps) in Prince Street, but it had always been residential rather than business premises.

The George Hotel, by the slipway, Prince Street. This was the first house in the town to call itself a hotel, rather than a mere inn, in around 1805.

Across the harbour from the North Pier. Note the 'dolphins', the cone-shaped constructions in the harbour on the left, which served as mooring posts for vessels when there was no room at the quayside. In the background on the right is Pool's Baths, built in a similar style to Bishop's defunct establishment on the sea front.

The Chicken Run Jetty. It was possibly so-named because of its metal framework. The jetty was built in 1904 on the site of the old South Pier.

North Pier repairs. Built in stone in 1816, but not completed until 1843, it replaced an earlier timber construction. In the background are the Victoria Rooms. The ship tied up is the *Majestic* of Lyme Regis, built in 1839.

The paddle steamer *Scarborough* nudges up to the North Pier to take on another load of passengers for a trip around the bay.

The Harbour Commissioners and the Harbour Master, 1924. Left to right: William Seager (Harbour Master), F. Strickland, D. Champlin, E. Nightingale, G. Hankinson, J. Mainprize, S. Charlesworth, G.Y. Lloyd Greame, W. Brown, C.F. Stonehouse, Alderman Hakes and Major Lawson. The commissioners were in charge of enforcing the collection of various tolls and duties, and used this money for the upkeep of the harbour. Their number was reduced from thirty to twenty-two after an Act of 1928; this, and the fact that the new commissioners were more dynamic than their predecessors, resulted in a great number of improvements.

The *Boy's Own*, Flamborough, 1938. This replaced another vessel, the *Girl's Own*, in that year. It was under the command of Captain James Newby. The *Boy's Own* returned to Bridlington after war service in 1945.

Harbour traffic, 1890s. The snow *Cholmley* had been built in Whitby in 1853, and was employed by her Newcastle owners on the coastal trade. A snow is a type of brig with a supplementary trysail mast.

Steam trawlers from Leith and Berwick-on-Tweed, Bridlington Harbour. Scottish, and to a lesser extent East Anglian, deep-sea herring boats put in to the harbour during the season, following the migrating shoals of fish. Scottish boats, sometimes as many as 100 at a time, were also in the habit of putting in on Sundays. Scottish trawlers made Bridlington their main base during 1899 and 1900.

Displaying the catch. The inshore trawling season for plaice ran from March to October, line fishing for cod ran from October to March; there was also drift fishing for herring. As well as fish there was a strong crab and lobster market from March to June.

A fish dealer and a carrier. Usually fish was landed at the fish market on the small Crane Jetty, but big boats, and in busy periods all craft, had to use the South Pier. In 1931 a special fish wharf and market was created at the seaward end of the South Pier.

The *Yorkshire Belle* off Flamborough Head, between the wars. She made her first appearance at Bridlington, replacing the *Britannia*. She was sunk during the war, but a new boat with the same name was built in 1948.

The RAF air/sea rescue launches, of which this is one, were housed in a shed, built in 1924, on Gummers Landing near the South Pier. They served the coastal gunnery and bombing ranges further down the coast off Skipsea. One of the men in the unit, during the late 1920s, was Lawrence of Arabia. The RAF presence continued until 1978, when the launches were superseded by helicopters.

Members of the Royal Yorkshire Yacht Club, 1922. The club was founded in 1847 and started an annual regatta in August 1904, which continues to the present day. The club also holds races throughout the summer months.

Yachts in full sail in the bay.

The greasy pole event formed part of the Aquatic Sports. These took place in the harbour as part of the annual carnival at the end of June.

The Aquatic Sports, 1920s. The sports were still going strong, although things are looking doubtful for the man on the right. In the centre background may be seen the top of a 'dolphin'.

The *Frenchman*. Paddles churning, and full of sightseers, she makes for the harbour entrance, for a trip around the bay. She was built as a tug named the *Coquet* in 1892 at South Shields, but was sold to Yorkshire owners, T. Gray (then the United Towing Co. of Hull) in 1899. She first appeared in Bridlington at Whitsun in 1922. The ship remained in service until 1928, before ending her days as a barge.

The *Yorkshireman*. Built in 1928 by Earle's of Hull, and also owned by United Towing, she comes into harbour on a very busy day, judging by the people waiting at the end of the pier. She remained in service until 1965, long after many of her competitors had retired. There were a number of boats which took people around Bridlington Bay: the *Scarborough*, the *Frenchman*, the *Yorkshireman*, the *Boy's Own*, the *Royal Jubilee* and the *Yorkshire Belle*.

Unknown fishermen. Note the different patterns on their guernseys: these particular patterns tend to be associated with North Riding ports such as Staithes, Robin Hood's Bay and Scarborough, and perhaps give a clue to their home town(s).

Bridlington Company, Boys' Naval Brigade, 1916. The Brigade was formed in late 1915 and commanded by Paymaster Francis Preston; he was assisted by Lieutenants Fewster and Wilson and Warrant Officers Robinson and Bishop (who was the drill instructor). The purpose of the Brigade was something like the Scouts or Naval Cadets, but was associated with the civilian pressure group the Navy League, rather than the Admiralty.

The harbour, 1928. Offshore are three destroyers, HMS *Valhalla*, *Wakefield* and *Wolverine*. They were present for the visit of Princess Mary.

Mr Browning, the much-decorated Chief
Officer of the Coastguard, *c*. 1879.

The old lifeboat, *George and Jane Walker*, came into service in 1899 and is seen here
being followed by its replacement, the *Stanhope Smart*, 1931. The RNLI took over an
existing private lifeboat in 1850, when the boat was housed in Chapel Street. It moved,
first to South Cliff and then, in 1904, to South Marine Drive.

Hauling the lifeboat ashore after a launch, 1920s. The boat was also launched in a similar manner: first nudged into the water by the tractor, a sail was raised and the wind was allowed to take her to sea.

Coxswain Hopper and the crew of the *George and Jane Walker*, 1922. This was the second lifeboat of this name in the town: the first, transferred from Barmston in 1898, was sold out of the service in 1899, without ever having been launched. The second lifeboat was, however, launched fifty-eight times in her career, and saved the lives of fifty mariners.

A rough sea. In the background Bridlington's first motor lifeboat, the *Stanhope Smart*, is standing by as the Grimsby fishing boat *Peggy* runs for the harbour. This lifeboat was launched sixty times between 1931 and 1947, and saved fifty-three lives.

The lifeboat *Seagull* in front of the Sailors' and Working Men's Clubhouse, Cliff Street. After the great gale of 1871, there was some dissatisfaction expressed at the performance of the town's two lifeboats, and the Revd Yarburgh Lloyd Greame donated this boat, to be owned by the club. It was badly damaged on 25 March 1898, going to the assistance of the brigantine *Lucinda*, and never sailed again.

The *Seagull*, in front of Fort Hall. The display was to raise money for the 'lifeboat sufferers Mrs C. Brown and R. Pickering'. The damage which the boat received while going to the aid of the *Lucinda* is clearly visible. One man (Christopher Brown) was killed; he was not even a member of the crew, although his son was. He had gone to the lifeboat's aid as it was being smashed against the sea wall and was swept out to sea after hauling three men ashore. Pickering broke his leg in the same incident. The boat was not built to RNLI standards, but was modelled on a South Shields pilot's boat.

THE NORTH SANDS

View from the North Pier, pre-1866. The sea defences consist merely of a sloping wooden barricade. The mock-Gothic Victoria Rooms are on the left.

View from the North Pier, 1880s. By this time the gardens, the sea wall and the new buildings along the sea front had all been developed.

Bishop's Improved Baths. They were built in 1844 to replace a previous structure of 1815. They offered 'all the modern improvements', with separate suites for men and women. The baths were closed in the 1860s with the opening of the Sea Wall (Royal Prince's) Parade.

The wooden sea defences. In the background are the Victoria Rooms and the North Pier. The rows of stumps visible near the waterline may mark the foundations of the original, wooden, North Pier.

Laying out the Sea Wall Parade, 1866. Viewed from the roof of the Victoria Rooms, the Alexandra Hotel can be seen in the background. Bishop's Baths are no more, but the chapel on the Esplanade is now visible. The latter belonged to the Primitive Methodists, and was built in 1833. It was no longer in use by 1866 and was demolished soon afterwards.

The side of the Victoria Rooms. The electrical plant for the building was concealed behind the mock castle walls in the background. Behind are the shops on Garrison Street, including John Rutter's, watchmakers.

The visit of Prince Albert Victor, Duke of Clarence, 20 July 1888. The Sea Wall Parade was renamed Royal Prince's Parade not, as the *Victoria County History* asserts, after a visit from Prince Albert (who had been dead for twenty-seven years by then), but after this visit by his son. The Prince's party is seen on the Parade, approaching the drawn up ranks of the 2nd Volunteer Battalion, East Yorkshire Regiment.

The same view, 1920s. The Floral and Grand Pavilions are in the background.

The Crescent. Built in 1869–71 by G.W. Travis of Sheffield, it was perhaps an attempt to bring a touch of Victorian elegance to the resort. The figures in the foreground have been touched in by a later hand.

The Parade, 1880s. Perhaps it is out of season, as everything is so quiet.

Entrance to the Parade, 1890s. Like the Spa Gardens, entrance was by ticket. As well as daily tickets, locals and holiday-makers staying for some length of time could also buy season tickets. Note the prams parked at the right: they could not go through the turnstiles, and had to be left outside.

The Esplanade, looking towards the harbour. The boys on the left appear to be selling something from their baskets, perhaps fish. Note the houses on the right, with their elegant balconies.

Prince's Parade and the Esplanade, 1890s.

The Floral Pavilion. People would gather to listen to a concert, or just to shelter from the sun and sea breezes. The pavilion was erected in 1904 near the bandstand. It now contains a ghost train.

The first Parade Band, 1876. They were led by Professor J.M. Wilson. The Local Government Board, the forerunner of the Borough Council, provided bands on the Parade from at least 1867, first on the bandstand and then in the Floral Pavilion.

Fred Rayne's North Regionals outside the Floral Pavilion. Fred Rayne is seated in the centre. The troupe received their name from the number of broadcasts that they made on the BBC's North Regional wireless station. They later changed their name to The Parade Show. At one time, one of the troupe was the young Beryl Reid, later to achieve fame on stage and screen.

Alfred Barker (front right) and his orchestra meet 'Mr Bridlington', the resort's entertainments manager, *c*. 1930. They are standing outside the Floral Pavilion. Barker was the Parade musical director in 1930. His orchestra, many members of which had played with the famous Hallé Orchestra, was 'one of the finest ever heard in Bridlington', according to a newspaper report.

The building of the Grand Pavilion, April 1906. The work is being done by S. Butler, a contractor from Stanningley, near Leeds.

The Grand Pavilion, arranged for a formal dinner. The Grand Pavilion was built in 1906, but was demolished and replaced by a boating lake in 1937, in order to maintain the view across the bay. A new Grand Pavilion was built in Victoria Terrace Gardens. Note the ornate ironwork under the balconies.

Unidentified pierrots, 1920s. Of all the troupes that performed in Bridlington, the Waterloos, led by the Beanland brothers, were perhaps the best known. Others included the Beaconsfield Singers, the White Musketeers, the Smart Set, the Vagabonds, the Brownies and the Idols, who continued the seaside tradition up to the Second World War.

The Royal Prince's Parade gates, August 1924. They are advertising Garadini and his orchestra; Garadini himself can be seen to the right. The Garadini Orchestra was one of those which made radio broadcasts from Hull during the 1920s. Other advertisements include one for the Grand Bijou Orchestra, conducted by Roland Rogers.

The demolition of the Grand Pavilion in November 1936. How many of the people watching its demolition had also watched its erection in 1906?

Fort Hall, which stood at the end of Fort Terrace. During the late eighteenth and early nineteenth centuries this was the town house of the Greame family of Sewerby Hall. It stood on or near the site of the fort that was built in 1667 to protect the harbour from the Dutch. It was demolished by the council in 1931 and is now the site of Leisure World. Since the house has rounded bay windows, it is possible that it was this house and that of the Boyntons on Manor Street (see page 34) which started the fashion for them in the town.

The Royal Prince's Parade extension, c. 1895. Later called the Victoria Wall, it was only a board-walk at this time, and a crowded board-walk at that. In the background, a troupe of pierrots are performing on a stage, and a carousel has been set up.

Sand art on the North Beach, 1920s. One of the drawings is of Flamborough church. The amount of patience and skill needed to complete such a display can only be imagined. Note the man at the water's edge carrying a harp. He may be from one of the many pierrot troupes who starred in the town.

What better souvenir of a day at the seaside than a photograph? The identity of this big group is not known, but there are so many present, it could well be a day out from a local village. The photograph possibly dates from the 1890s.

This beach photographer worked for Mr Snaps. The firm had premises at the end of Prince Street and on the Promenade.

A prize-winning sandcastle. The team of four constructed a model of the harbour – though the purist might say that this is not a castle as such. Such a competition formed part of the annual carnival. Note how the girls have the spades, while the boys are just sitting down!

Victoria Terrace Gardens, *c.* 1924. This is the site of the second Grand Pavilion on the east side of the Promenade. It is a gloomy winter's day but there is still plenty going on in the town. The posters reveal recitals, dances and a panto. The house on the left was used as a boarding-house for the High School.

Burgin's Fun City, an early amusement arcade, 1923. Among the booths inside are 'The Wobbling Tanks: the latest game of skill' and Madame Psycho ABIMS, palmist and clairvoyant. There was also a 'wireless telegraph' for the public to use. Comments in the newspapers at the time suggest that people considered it rather common. The building is still there, just south of the Expanse Hotel, but has been altered by the addition of a pantile roof.

Beaconsfield Sea Wall. It was completed in 1888. The sign on the left, permitting only pedestrians and bath chairs, has obviously not deterred the owner of the car.

North Sands, near the end of Prince's Parade and the beginning of the Beaconsfield Sea Wall. Note the sign for 'mixed bathing', painted on the sea wall in the background. The woman in the centre appears to be sitting on a kind of wheeled deck-chair.

More beach excavations. It may be summer and sunny, but these two girls, and the poor boy in the Norfolk jacket in the background, are proof against anything the weather might produce, hot or cold.

The tennis courts, Beaconsfield public gardens, *c.* 1935. The end of the gardens nearest the sea had once contained a big pavilion, where the Waterloo Pierrots gave evening performances. The gardens were later turned into a bowling green, and are now a car park.

Horse and carriage outside the new Floral Hall. It was built in 1921 but is now the site of a car park.

The cast of the revue *How Time Flies* outside the Floral Hall. According to local newspaper reports, it opened on 2 July 1924 to a 'large and appreciative audience'. The director was P. Selwyn Newbound, and the cast included Ewart Scott (light comedian), Thelma Dane (contralto), Bret Hayden (entertainer and mime) and Juliette de Gai ('Parisien danseuse'), as well as 'a bevy of beautiful girls'.

The Floral Hall, August 1924. The fire destroyed the hall after only three years. Anyone who wanted to see the popular star George Robey, who was known as 'The Prime Minister of Mirth', would have been disappointed.

Donkeys below Beaconsfield Sea Wall. Introduced to Bridlington in 1896, donkeys are now a traditional part of the seaside scene.

'Children's Corner', North Beach, *c.* 1900. A group of pierrots entertain the crowd. This could well be the Waterloo troupe, judging by their costumes; they certainly included a harpist, who can be seen at the rear of the stage. They have attracted a big crowd and the ice cream stand in the foreground is no doubt doing good business.

Mine damage, 1 May 1918. A mine came adrift from one of the minefields laid by the British and German navies in the North Sea over the preceding four years. Despite the best efforts of police and coastguard, it drifted ashore near Trinity Cut, and, presumably striking a rock, exploded. The damage to the houses and hotels along the sea front was estimated as some £2–3,000, but fortunately no one was seriously injured.

North Sands. Note the bathing machines at the water's edge. By 1908, owners paid 5s per van for using the beach. In 1907 bathing without vans was only permitted on three specified areas of the beach: one for men only, one for women only and one for mixed bathing. Even then it was only allowed before 8 a.m. The contraption on the right is providing rope slides for the more daring children.

'Bathing women'. Mrs Bullock and Mrs Welbourne looked after women using the bathing vans. They are carrying their cleaning equipment, and are both wearing stout shoes.

The bridge over Trinity Cut, originally called Sands Cut, was built in 1888. In the background is the Alexandra Hydro Hotel, built in 1863–6 on what was then called Sewerby Terrace, but was later renamed Alexandra Terrace. It was once one of the finest hotels in England, but has since been demolished; the site is now occupied by flats.

Storm damage to the sea wall. The three people sitting at the bottom are H.S. Blundell, Mrs Fisher and 'Uncle William'.

North Sands from Trinity Cut bridge. Wilson's Private Boarding House later became a nursing home called Danes Lea, and then, from 1951, a residential home. Just visible among the trees in the background is Sewerby vicarage, now a hotel.

The Switchback Railway, Sands Lane, 1892. The entrance fee was 2*d*. A bit tame by today's standards perhaps, it was built in 1890 and was demolished in 1912.

The Switchback Railway. Just leaving is a convoy of Wolds wagons – no doubt a day trip from one of the nearby towns or villages. Trips to the coast were an important part of the year in country villages, and the wagons and harness were often heavily decorated for the occasion with flowers and ribbons.

Sewerby Cliffs. The men of the Bridlington Rocket Company demonstrate a rescue by breeches buoy. The company enabled rescues to be made from ships driven ashore, where the lifeboat could not get close enough.

Outside the gates of Sewerby Hall, *c.* 1910. On the right is the village post office, with the postman, or possibly even George Chadwick, the postmaster, standing in the door. A telegraph lad is poised on his bike, even though this was not a telegraph office.

A decorated cart, possibly for the Empire Day celebrations at Flamborough, 1907.

The funeral of three fishermen, Flamborough, 8 February 1909. The men, Tom Major and Richard and John Cross, were drowned when the Crosses' coble *Gleaner* capsized off West Scar Rocks on the north side of the Head. Major's boat, the *Two Brothers*, went to their rescue, but suffered a similar fate. Altogether six men, the crews of both boats, were drowned. As many as 5,000 people, some from as far away as Hull, came to the funeral. A monument was later erected by public subscription. The musicians are from the Green Howards: Richard Cross and Tom Major were both in the Territorial Army and so were given a military funeral.

Acknowledgements

We should like to thank Humberside Leisure Services for their co-operation in the provision of the pictures; and to thank the following for their help:

Chrys Mellor • Jane Wilshere • the staff of Bridlington Public Library
the staff of Beverley Reference Library • the staff of Hull Technical Library
the staff of Grimsby Reference Library • Chris Ketchell

Looking south-west towards Bridlington, with the Priory in the distance. No record has been found of the tower on the left.

BRITAIN IN OLD PHOTOGRAPHS

To order any of these titles please telephone Littlehampton Book Services on 01903 721596

ALDERNEY

Alderney: A Second Selection, *B Bonnard*

BEDFORDSHIRE

Bedfordshire at Work, *N Lutt*

BERKSHIRE

Maidenhead, *M Hayles & D Hedges*
Around Maidenhead, *M Hayles & B Hedges*
Reading, *P Southerton*
Reading: A Second Selection, *P Southerton*
Sandhurst and Crowthorne, *K Dancy*
Around Slough, *J Hunter & K Hunter*
Around Thatcham, *P Allen*
Around Windsor, *B Hedges*

BUCKINGHAMSHIRE

Buckingham and District, *R Cook*
High Wycombe, *R Goodearl*
Around Stony Stratford, *A Lambert*

CHESHIRE

Cheshire Railways, *M Hitches*
Chester, *S Nichols*

CLWYD

Clwyd Railways, *M Hitches*

CLYDESDALE

Clydesdale, *Lesmahagow Parish Historical Association*

CORNWALL

Cornish Coast, *T Bowden*
Falmouth, *P Gilson*
Lower Fal, *P Gilson*
Around Padstow, *M McCarthy*
Around Penzance, *J Holmes*
Penzance and Newlyn, *J Holmes*
Around Truro, *A Lyne*
Upper Fal, *P Gilson*

CUMBERLAND

Cockermouth and District, *J Bernard Bradbury*
Keswick and the Central Lakes, *J Marsh*
Around Penrith, *F Boyd*
Around Whitehaven, *H Fancy*

DERBYSHIRE

Derby, *D Buxton*
Around Matlock, *D Barton*

DEVON

Colyton and Seaton, *T Gosling*
Dawlish and Teignmouth, *G Gosling*
Devon Aerodromes, *K Saunders*
Exeter, *P Thomas*
Exmouth and Budleigh Salterton, *T Gosling*
From Haldon to Mid-Dartmoor, *J Hall*
Honiton and the Otter Valley, *J Yallop*
Around Kingsbridge, *K Tanner*
Around Seaton and Sidmouth, *T Gosling*
Seaton, Axminster and Lyme Regis, *T Gosling*

DORSET

Around Blandford Forum, *B Cox*
Bournemouth, *M Colman*
Bridport and the Bride Valley, *J Burrell & S Humphries*
Dorchester, *T Gosling*
Around Gillingham, *P Crocker*

DURHAM

Darlington, *G Flynn*
Darlington: A Second Selection, *G Flynn*
Durham People, *M Richardson*
Houghton-le-Spring and Hetton-le-Hole, *K Richardson*
Houghton-le-Spring and Hetton-le-Hole:
  A Second Selection, *K Richardson*
Sunderland, *S Miller & B Bell*
Teesdale, *D Coggins*
Teesdale: A Second Selection, *P Raine*
Weardale, *J Crosby*
Weardale: A Second Selection, *J Crosby*

DYFED

Aberystwyth and North Ceredigion,
  Dyfed Cultural Services Dept
Haverfordwest, *Dyfed Cultural Services Dept*
Upper Tywi Valley, *Dyfed Cultural Services Dept*

ESSEX

Around Grays, *B Evans*

GLOUCESTERSHIRE

Along the Avon from Stratford to Tewkesbury, *J Jeremiah*
Cheltenham: A Second Selection, *R Whiting*
Cheltenham at War, *P Gill*
Cirencester, *J Welsford*
Around Cirencester, *E Cuss & P Griffiths*
Forest, The, *D Mullin*
Gloucester, *J Voyce*
Around Gloucester, *A Sutton*
Gloucester: From the Walwin Collection, *J Voyce*
North Cotswolds, *D Viner*
Severn Vale, *A Sutton*
Stonehouse to Painswick, *A Sutton*
Stroud and the Five Valleys, *S Gardiner & L Padin*
Stroud and the Five Valleys: A Second Selection,
  S Gardiner & L Padin
Stroud's Golden Valley, *S Gardiner & L Padin*
Stroudwater and Thames & Severn Canals,
  E Cuss & S Gardiner
Stroudwater and Thames & Severn Canals: A Second
  Selection, *E Cuss & S Gardiner*
Tewkesbury and the Vale of Gloucester, *C Hilton*
Thornbury to Berkeley, *J Hudson*
Uley, Dursley and Cam, *A Sutton*
Wotton-under-Edge to Chipping Sodbury, *A Sutton*

GWYNEDD

Anglesey, *M Hitches*
Gwynedd Railways, *M Hitches*
Around Llandudno, *M Hitches*
Vale of Conwy, *M Hitches*

HAMPSHIRE

Gosport, *J Sadden*
Portsmouth, *P Rogers & D Francis*

HEREFORDSHIRE

Herefordshire, *A Sandford*

HERTFORDSHIRE

Barnet, *I Norrie*
Hitchin, *A Fleck*
St Albans, *S Mullins*
Stevenage, *M Appleton*

ISLE OF MAN

The Tourist Trophy, *B Snelling*

ISLE OF WIGHT

Newport, *D Parr*
Around Ryde, *D Parr*

JERSEY

Jersey: A Third Selection, *R Lemprière*

KENT

Bexley, *M Scott*
Broadstairs and St Peter's, *J Whyman*
Bromley, Keston and Hayes, *M Scott*
Canterbury: A Second Selection, *D Butler*
Chatham and Gillingham, *P MacDougall*
Chatham Dockyard, *P MacDougall*
Deal, *J Broady*
Early Broadstairs and St Peter's, *B Wootton*
East Kent at War, *D Collyer*
Eltham, *J Kennett*
Folkestone: A Second Selection, *A Taylor & E Rooney*
Goudhurst to Tenterden, *A Guilmant*
Gravesend, *R Hiscock*
Around Gravesham, *R Hiscock & D Grierson*
Herne Bay, *J Hawkins*
Lympne Airport, *D Collyer*
Maidstone, *I Hales*
Margate, *R Clements*
RAF Hawkinge, *R Humphreys*
RAF Manston, *RAF Manston History Club*
RAF Manston: A Second Selection,
  RAF Manston History Club
Ramsgate and Thanet Life, *D Perkins*
Romney Marsh, *E Carpenter*
Sandwich, *C Wanostrocht*
Around Tonbridge, *C Bell*
Tunbridge Wells, *M Rowlands & I Beavis*
Tunbridge Wells: A Second Selection,
  M Rowlands & I Beavis
Around Whitstable, *C Court*
Wingham, Adisham and Littlebourne, *M Crane*

LANCASHIRE

Around Barrow-in-Furness, *J Garbutt & J Marsh*
Blackpool, *C Rothwell*
Bury, *J Hudson*
Chorley and District, *J Smith*
Fleetwood, *C Rothwell*
Heywood, *J Hudson*
Around Kirkham, *C Rothwell*
Lancashire North of the Sands, *J Garbutt & J Marsh*
Around Lancaster, *S Ashworth*
Lytham St Anne's, *C Rothwell*
North Fylde, *C Rothwell*
Radcliffe, *J Hudson*
Rossendale, *B Moore & N Dunnachie*

LEICESTERSHIRE

Around Ashby-de-la-Zouch, *K Hillier*
Charnwood Forest, *I Keil, W Humphrey & D Wix*
Leicester, *D Burton*
Leicester: A Second Selection, *D Burton*
Melton Mowbray, *T Hickman*
Around Melton Mowbray, *T Hickman*
River Soar, *D Wix, P Shacklock & I Keil*
Rutland, *T Clough*
Vale of Belvoir, *T Hickman*
Around the Welland Valley, *S Mastoris*

LINCOLNSHIRE

Grimsby, *J Tierney*
Around Grimsby, *J Tierney*
Grimsby Docks, *J Tierney*
Lincoln, *D Cuppleditch*